"No matter what line of work you're in, whether it be guiding clients to the summit of Mt. Everest or selling real estate, the same values get you to the top: Honesty, hard work, attention to detail, inspiration, and focus.

Having scaled the tallest peak in the Americas at nearly 23,000ft in the Andes with Matt Parker, and having hired his real estate services, I can attest that he exhibits these traits regardless of the endeavor. Parker's focus on providing me with a positive real estate experience was the same focus that drove him through the thin air and punishing summit day of Aconcagua to stand on the highest point in the Americas."

– **Michael Hamill**, Professional Mountain Guide, Author, *Climbing the Seven Summits*

What is your mountain?

The Real Estate Sales Secret
What Top Real Estate Listing Agents Do Today To Sell Tomorrow

ISBN: 9780996300926

THE REAL ESTATE
SALES
SECRET

WHAT TOP REAL ESTATE LISTING
AGENTS DO TODAY TO SELL TOMORROW

Download powerful listing
and sales tools at:

www.mattcparker.com

Foreward

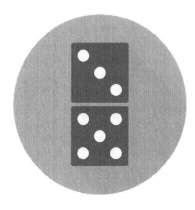

Twelve months prior, the 11" long fresh scar was unimaginable on the top of her head. Previously, she had jet black hair, even in her late 60's, and a distinctive Audrey Hepburn look. Despite the archaic qualities of years-old family photographs in her home, Grandma Cris displayed a timeless sex appeal and serene happiness in them.

Terminal brain cancer stages a brutal physical attack on it's victims. It's a maddening hurricane force storm of constant surgeries, drugs and nausea. Daily, this assault was drawing the life from Grandma Cris with physical repercussions too painful to write. The least of these was her ability to speak.

Despite the aggression of her cancer, Grandma Cris could play dominoes. Play dominoes, walk and enjoy Chicago Bulls games. One or two times a week, I would drive or walk to their home, knock on the door, hold her by her arm and walk her to the refrigerator. On the refrigerator she posted a pencil-written dominoes tally on a small piece of note paper. We moved a refrigerator magnet, grabbed the paper, sat down at the dining room table and played silent dominoes. The silence was broken only by the subtle sound of her lips cracking when she smiled. No speaking, still a smile.

When we were done, we would walk up their steep wooded driveway to the street, look left and then turn and walk past multiple barking dogs around the neighborhood block. After our last game of dominoes, our last walk, I remember losing to someone who couldn't really function. She died on a win. The Chicago Bulls probably inspired her.

There are many great real estate agents in this world by many measures. I have learned from many of them and will not engage in a debate regarding whom amongst them is the best. Further, I will not judge my own performance against you, my peers and associates for whom I have high respect and with whom I share a kindred drive and spirit. Objectively speaking, the following is true to the best of my knowledge: I have been, and am, routinely in the top zero to five percent of real estate agents in the United States as measured by commission production. I'd prefer that were private.

I have been, and am, one of the leading real estate agents in my small little corner of the world south of Seattle, Washington. Many agents in and around Seattle are far more important than I am.

I have had the pleasure of being voted one of the top agents in my city multiple times starting in my twenties. I have, with a great business partner, gone nearly two years and signed every customer I interviewed with using the steps outlined in this book. I am not Warren Buffet and do not have my own television show.

Despite any accomplishments, or lack of them, many people have and will make far more commissions and sales than I ever have or ever will. To me, though, sales are apples off a more important tree.

I have measured my success in freedom, the freedom to stop work at any time to play dominoes. **In attaining my own freedom, a vibrant life, the confidence to smile everyday and turn my phone off—I am absolutely an expert.** This is what I would rather you know about me.

"How do I measure my success? How do I smile everyday? How do I stay fit? How do I NEVER choose work over a family members need? (Grandma Cris died before I sold any real estate, but the need for freedom to help family lodged itself in my mind)." These are far better questions than, "How many houses can I sell? How do I absolutely maximize my gross commissionable income? Did I trump all of my peers?"

The first questions are the important ones. The beauty of real estate brokerage is that success in this field is compatible with answering important questions. Living a great, happy and healthy life is easily blended with selling award-winning amounts of real estate.

Great real estate agents leave breadcrumbs, clues, down the path to treasure. These clues reveal values, virtues and practices that are simple, efficient and effective. The vital clue in its purest language is provided here for you to execute today.

You can live a free, healthy and vibrant life selling real estate. I have succeeded in this, and would compete against anyone in this field of categories, the important ones. Your dreams can be actualized by selling real estate. Please read this book, implement the method and call me when you need inspiration.

I have made it important to have time to answer you, to play dominoes. This book *is not* about my resume, *it is* about you and your dreams.

For my mom, dad, brother, and uncle.

ACKNOWLEDGMENTS

Thank you to principled, excited, kind, and risk-taking individuals whom have gifted me their time, tactics and training: Coach Kniestedt, Coach Willis, Captain Doug,
Kevin Younkin, Mitchell Chase, Barry Crittenden, Ann Rule, Dustin Keeth, Gary Keeth, Chad Ohrt, Dan Nieder, Phil Ershler, Michael Hamill, Tammy Burmeister, Brent Saxwold,
Elliot Trotter, Rocky Kimball PhD and Jim McCullen.

Their lessons are the thread of this project.

Thanks also to my adventure teammates:
Justin, Joe, Joey, Kali, Remick and Chris.

Table of Contents

Section 1: Preliminary Listing Interaction

Part I: Mind-Set

Part II: - First Phone Call

Part III: The Walk-Through

Part IV: Second Phone Call

Section 2: The Listing Presentation

Part V: Listing Presentation Preparation

Part VI: The Price Presentation

Part VII: Giving the Listing Presentation:
The Marketing Presentation

Part VIII: Giving the Listing Presentation:
My Résumé Presentation

Seventy-Three Dollars
Per Minute

You have the pedigree and the natural skills to be successful today. Never forget you are the successful product of a harsh universe; the simple fact that you exist, whence trillions of other organisms do not, is a mathematical miracle. The cells in your body pulse with inherent success.

The material in this book is not contained or explained in any other real estate sales book or publication. Like you, it is totally unique. Additionally, the material in this book is inseparable from your distinct natural ability to physically create your dreams. This publication, and your specific execution of it, is a one-of-a-kind personal process of triumph.

Listing and selling real estate is simple, within your reach, and possible today. You do not need postcards, client lists or paid internet advertisements to sign a contract that will pay you $45,000 in thirty days.

This book will answer the following important questions:

- How do I unleash my primal, distinct and unique ability to sell?
- How do I jumpstart my entire real estate business?
- How do I sign a listing today?
- What simple thing wins the listing?
- How do I win the listing against a great agent?
- Which of the many distractions of real estate can I eliminate?
- How do I create a stream of listings and sales?

Any plan you have to become a viable real estate broker must start with a single listing that sells, the same way an ocean starts with a drop of water. Your ability to sign and sell a listing is wholly determined upon successfully executing the home walk-through and listing presentation. Together, these take ninety minutes. You earn $73 per minute in these ninety minutes[1]. Per *minute*, not per hour. **You make or break your real estate career in these ninety minutes.**

That's $168 per minute in San Diego[2], where residential real estate prices are the fourth highest in the nation[3]. or $15,000 per ninety minutes. That's $52 per minute in Cedar Rapids, Iowa[4] or $4,680 per ninety minutes.

---

1   Based on 3 percent commission paid on a median home price of $504,200. Price/minute determined using ninety-minute sessions (two forty-five-minute meetings). National Association of Realtors (NAR), "Median Sales Price of Existing Single-Family Homes for Metropolitan Areas," accessed March 2015, http://www.realtor.org/topics/metropolitan-median-area-prices-and-affordability/data.

2,4   NAR, "Median Sales Price of Existing Single-Family Homes for Metropolitan Areas," accessed March 2015, http://www.realtor.org/topics/metropolitan-median-area-prices-and-affordability/data.

3   Based on 3 percent commission paid on a median home price of $156,300 Price/minute determined using ninety-minute sessions (two forty-five-minute meetings). National Association of Realtors (NAR), "Median Sales Price of Existing Single-Family Homes for Metropolitan Areas," accessed March 2015, http://www.realtor.org/topics/metropolitan-median-area-prices-and-affordability/data.

Use this book as a checklist, marking it and taking notes as a quarterback to his playbook anytime you have the any chance of signing a seller to a listing contract. Your specific, individual answers to these questions are integral to exposing and using your unique inborn talent to dutifully serve your peers.

What's the catch?

First, you must *need*, not *want*, success. If you *want* success, take a number and stand in line with everyone else on this planet. If you truly need success, you will be successful.

Second, you must own the following mind-set: *your need to succeed must be aligned with the customer succeeding; for you to succeed, your customer must succeed*. You can achieve short-term success at the expense of others. Avoid this; it is temporary. No matter what your political, social, or religious beliefs, this will ultimately poison your social ecosystem and eventually your own mental state.

> *"Do not try to get success from something that is wrong...If your thinking is wrong, it is wrong and not right and can never be right so long as it is wrong. If it is wrong in essence, it is bound to be wrong in the result."*
>
> — **Norman Vincent Peale**, The Power of Positive Thinking

You need not unlock a guarded door to the treasure room of great prosperity; your own precious resources, your innate skills, are all you need. Signing and selling a listing is a simple process initiated in ninety minutes when you follow the steps contained herein by answering these personal, powerful questions.

SECTION
ONE

Preliminary
Listing
Interaction

PART I
MINDSET

Why?

Ask a drowning man what he needs.

Without doubt, his reply is:

"Air."

What do I need? For what do I strive? What am I doing here today? Why I am doing this?

Much is made of chasing these questions. The answer is not atop a high mountain, nor encrypted in the writings of great spiritual leaders. The answers to these questions are mine and easily within my reach. *I* own the answers, not a distant institution. Like the man who needs air, when I am forced to identify my goals, they immediately answer my call. I know what I need now, immediately. My needs, visions, and goals are my life force, and they are here now, today, and easily within my reach. I wither and perish when I have no purpose.

In a single moment I can tell you what my goals are. I can speak them. I can write them. I can present them in drawings, photos, and metaphors. *The medium is not important.*

The goals themselves are of upmost importance! What can be more important than that which dictates all actions in my life? With no destination in mind, I end up nowhere. This is not a surprise.

I have clear goals.

I have clear goals. **This means I know *exactly* what I need and *when* I will get it.** All successful endeavors in this universe, all of them, begin with a dream, a vision…a goal! I accept that I will not be successful without proclamation of my goals. It is impossible for me or any living thing to succeed without a definition of success. This definition, collectively, is my goal.

Does the lion know for what he waits?

The antelope, of course!

Could he not visualize the antelope, when it arrived, he would not know what to do.

When the lion sees the antelope, it is predetermined that he gives chase.

I have clear goals. I will succeed. If I have not proclaimed my goals, I will not read another page until I have. They may be grand, small, material, or immaterial—it doesn't matter—but I will render my goals on paper, in pictures, or in conversation with my peers. I hereby proclaim my goals, privately or publicly.

My goals are not perfect, and I do not know exactly how I will achieve them. I don't care; **I have clear goals**. This I know; this I have proclaimed. I hereby ascribe to the great nonsecret of success, that goals beget achievement. I have clear goals.

The lion knows what he hunts. I know my goals.

Do I *need* to do this?

I *need* my goals accomplished. Not "want."

NEED.

This distinction is of paramount importance.

I will lie on my deathbed sad and meager if I do not attain my goals in life.

Everyone *wants* love, purpose, and freedom. No matter what we disagree on, we all agree on these.

Only those who *need* the gifts of the earth receive them. Those who need, commit. I *need* my goals achieved, so I am committed to achieving them.

The raindrop is committed to reaching the sea. Nothing will stop the raindrop, nothing. It may take a single day, or years, but the rain inevitably joins the sea. I am a raindrop driven to the sea.

Just try to stop me.

Embarrassment? I cannot be embarrassed. How can I be embarrassed to fulfill a life of wonderful joy?

Fear? Thank goodness I am afraid! This gives me energy, creativity, and strength.

Confusion? This leads me to exploration, where all answers are found.

I am committed. Those things that stop my peers are mere obstacles to me. I bludgeon each obstacle, and it strengthens my commitment. My peers say:

"How did he do that?"

They think I have a powerful secret ring in my pocket!

I do. **The secret ring is commitment.** I *need* the great riches the heavens offer me during this, my one short pass on this planet. I am committed to achieving my goals. No worldly force will stand in my way.

I am committed to my goals. I **need** my goals accomplished.

Just try to stop me.

How?

I will cast this book away into a dark corner until I have taken my goals and vocation to the altar and married them. I will succeed at my vocation and achieve my goals because I have earned the time, freedom, resources, and influence to attain anything I need.

My goals will be achieved through my vocation, through listing and selling real estate.

This irrevocable marriage, my goals to my vocation, is absolutely mandatory. I may sell for a month, a year, or ten years, but this is my vocation now, so I will achieve all of my earthly goals through success in my vocation.

My goal is to feed my child the finest meal. To list real estate successfully is to feed my child.

What happens when despair stands in my way? I immediately remember that I toil to feed my child! **I cannot fail.**

My goal is to save my body from extended years of physically destructive manual labor.

I know to successfully list real estate is to protect my physical being. **I will overwhelm my obstacles, because I must to stay alive!**

My goals and my desire to successfully list real estate are the same thing; this is my proof that nothing will stand in the way of my success. I hereby irreversibly connect my goals and my pursuit to successfully list real estate. Now, my success is guaranteed.

If I cannot achieve my goals through selling real estate, why would I choose this profession? Many professions offer far less risk and far less reward.

If my dream is to run, I do not jump in the river.

If my dream is to fly, I spread my wings.

For a vocation with literally limitless potential, I have traded the ruse of comfort. My children will eat from the bountiful harvest of my labors, plucking ripe, golden apples from the tree. They will not scavenge the floor for what animals have passed by.

My dreams may include early retirement on a tropical island, cycling the South American continent, or simply putting food on my child's plate, but the next step to my dreams will be achieved through listing real estate. Today.

If my dreams cannot be actualized through listing real estate, I am putting this book down and figuring out how I will achieve my dreams.

My visions, dreams, and goals will be accomplished through listing real estate.

Because of this marriage, this spiritual synergy, my powers are twice that of my competition.

PART II

FIRST
PHONE
CALL

Who?

I wake and watch the clock. I sit and see the seconds hand on the clock tick to the right:

Tick. Tick. Tick.

Slowly, it seems, the ticking of the clock continues.

Tick. Tick. Tick.

Each *tick* of the clock is gone forever, never to be replaced, lost to the ages.

Tick. Tick. Tick.

I have been gifted a limited number of *ticks* in my life. When the clock—

BONG! BONG! BONG!

When the clock finally *BONGS*, my time is gone forever. I will be cold to the earth, gone, never to return to this life and hold my family in their earthly forms.

My time on this planet is limited; therefore, it is priceless. This is the definition of *priceless*. By luck, I am the banker of my own precious vault of golden time. **I will not waste a *tick*. Not one.**

I am speaking to the decision maker and only to the decision maker.

His associate, his neighbor, and his friend, wanting for an open ear, will talk at me. They will attempt to fill my hours with challenges I am not qualified to solve. They will gush endless opinions, dialogue, and drama. **I am concerned with this type of conversation only with my precious loved ones.** At work, all conversation with anyone but the decision maker is my own gold slipping out of my hands—it is my priceless resource squandered, washed down the drain.

I choose to speak only to the decision maker.

There are infinite riches in this world for me. No savage ruler has ever seen the limits of the world's wealth. I need but a small slice of this endless resource, but I have a specific time limit in which to gain it. I will not deplete my precious vault of time for the grand line of time wasters. *I will speak only to he who can clothe my family.*

I will talk only to decision makers. **Then, they will make decisions!**

I am focused on the decision maker today, and no one else.

I am in charge of the most important bank in the universe, and *I* decide how to spend the most precious resource.

What is the most important question in real estate brokerage?

"Would you like to sign now?"

Seven words can save me seven thousand words.

"Would you like to sign now?"

No bone has ever been broken as a result of this question!

"Would you like to sign now?" I ask.

"Yes!" my customer says.

I have a listing!

If my customer has decided to use me, and I do *not* ask this question, what happens?

The open door may be closed, as all doors do.

"Would you like to sign now?"

If they are not ready, my customer says no, and we proceed with no broken bones.

They may be ready, of course, and so will I!

If my customer is ready to sign, I will sign him. Period. All of the time, in all conditions, under any moon.

If my customer will sign, I will sign him.

I have asked my customer, "Would you like to sign the paperwork now?"

Maybe he says yes.

And just like that, my dreams are realized.

How long is the walk-through?

How much time *could* we spend at my customer's house?

They live there...

There is no limit to how long we could visit! The customer is at home when I arrive, at home when I am there, and will be at home when I am gone. I could spend all morning, all day, and even all night at their house! Where is the line drawn that I have overstayed my welcome?

Forty-five minutes.

I know this home is constructed of wood, mortar, and emotion. The walls of this home pulse with hundreds of thousands of moments and memories. It's best these feelings be kept in the walls, for if I tap into them, they will overflow into our meeting, drowning our professional conversation! If I indulge in a long, emotional meeting, I will wade through the halls of emotion with my customer.

When I accomplish my walk-through in forty-five minutes, my customer and I will deliberate on rational, functional, and strategic topics—the fundamental pillars of our successful engagement.

We will not drown in emotion, killing our successful sale. I will leave the walk-through dry and happy.

My customer knows the walk-through takes no more than forty-five minutes. I have told him or her this before I reach the house. My customer knows that at forty-five minutes, I must leave for my next meeting.

Shame on me if I knowingly flood my customer with emotion while we're in his or her home.

My customer and I have agreed to a **forty-five-minute** walk-through. No more. I will not unleash a spring of emotion for my customer by making the walk through arduous and personal. It will be forty-five minutes, and it will be professional. This is what my customer wants, and this is how we will succeed.

If I want to drown, I will consciously engage in a prolonged, personal walk-through. Here is my plan for stress, deception, fatigue, and failure.

My plan for success is a forty-five-minute professional walk-through.

PART III

THE WALKTHROUGH

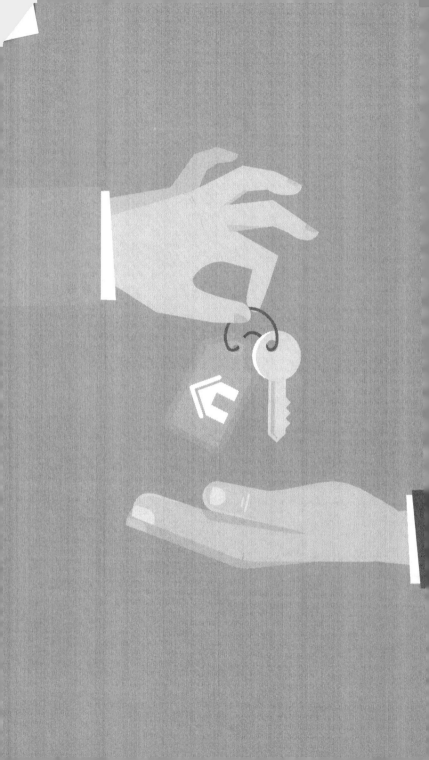

What topic is taboo in the customer's home?

Me.

There is nothing in my customer's life she does not bring home in some fashion:

Her child, her lover, and her parents.

Her sweat, her smell, and her habits.

Her soiled clothing, her gold, and her trophies.

Whether physically or emotionally, ALL of my customer's life comes to rest in her home. **All of it.** For even the most confident, social individual, this makes the home a private, self-conscious place. Is not the United States founded on principles that such a place be kept private?

My customer brings everything home.

Then, she brings me there.

The place she does *not* bring any other professional and many of her friends is opened to *me*? **Her door is locked to the world, but opened to me?**

I am humbled. I am aware that I have been given a rare chance to enter my customer's home, where she is highly, highly self-conscious. Accordingly, her ears are rightfully sealed to *my* story. All topics related to "me" are taboo. All topics related to "me" are understandably blocked by my customer's mind; her mind is locked in a state of self-consciousness.

At home, the customer cares not where I came from, what I drive, or even what sales awards I've won. These will matter in time, later. Currently, she is only interested in her needs that her privacy is considered sacred and her life shown respect.

I will speak little, and query lots! I will not pass judgment. I will not talk about myself. I will give my opinion briefly and only when asked.

I will not, under any circumstances, imply her countertops are inadequate! In her home, the countertops are layered with myriad memories; how can I quantify the value of her life's memories?

I cannot. Again, my strategic opinions are of little import at this time. Right now, they will be considered heartless attacks on her life. I will show nothing but love, admiration, and respect for her home under any circumstances and *despite any condition the home is in.*

This key, forged of humility and respect, will unlock her heart to the pursuit of an honest salesperson. **My competitor, no matter his prowess, cannot unlock the door to the customer's trust with arrogance.** I will abandon my ego, demonstrate true concern, and win the chance to feed myself.

I will show concern only for my customer, and nothing else. I will not talk about "me."

What is the one thing I must ascertain at the walk-through?

I am not leaving this home until I know *why the customer thinks it won't sell.*

Not why *I* think it won't sell—**why *the customer* thinks it won't sell.**

This is the most precious piece of information I will gather at the walk-through.

"Sir, why won't your house sell?"

I can see the paint peeling. I can smell the pet odor. I can see the crack in the foundation. *These are of no import to our discussions at the walk-through, though they will be important later.*

The seller's love for his home has blinded him to these defects! Now is not the time to discuss these; now is the time to ask him why *he* thinks his home won't sell.

The answer to this question is universally important to successful listing brokers.

When I know what the seller thinks will hold him back, only then can I help him. This is the very definition of a sale.

The odds of randomly addressing his primary concern are negligible, if not nonexistent. **How can I sell someone my service if my service doesn't address his fear?**

Only by luck, and my business will not be built on luck alone!

Every seller cares about price.

Every seller cares about commission.

It is also true every seller, no matter how confident, is worried that his home won't sell. He will bluff, and he will puff out his chest and exclaim:

"I am not worried about my house selling."

This is the first sign that they ARE worried about their house selling!

"Sir, why won't your house sell?"

This is the most important question I will address at the walk-through.

There are myriad responses to it. Once I know the answer, I have the information I need to deliver a successful listing presentation. Before asking this question, I know less about the seller's thought process than his cat does.

When I address what the seller is worried about, he will have unshakeable confidence in my ability to listen, interpret, analyze, and execute. My professionalism will turn from that of a minion to that of a general.

He will follow my lead.

What notes are vital to take at the walk-through?

Can a family with seven dogs remove 100 percent of the pet odor? No.

Can a golfer who practices daily in his yard keep his grass immaculate? No.

Can an organic gardener keep her yard and home insect free? No.

I am not leaving this home without knowing what needs to be, and *can be*, completed before we list it. I will write this on a clipboard during the walk-through.

Occasionally, I will get lucky, and the customer will have a turnkey home. If that is the case, I can move on from this step. If that is not the case, I will assess what needs to be done, and whether it *can be* done or not.

Every customer has a different capacity to accomplish work orders. I recognize this. If I see four potential listing preparation tasks, I will assess whether or not the customer can do these things in a reasonable amount of time, with a limited amount of resources and effort.

What do I tell the doctor who tells me to give up my favorite food? *I choose a new doctor!*

y walk-through I will discern what needs to be, and *can be*, done. This is easy and intuitive. Later, my pricing presentation will include work orders for the seller. These could include reasonable referrals to contractors who can efficiently help them. If the customer can't accomplish or heed my advice, I will not suggest a task! I will not ask a lion to play the guitar.

My customers cannot jump out of their skin to accomplish otherworldly feats of home preparation, so I will not give this stress to them. If I do, I will make the process too hard for them, and we will fail to even get the house on the market.

I will not leave the walk-through without knowing what the customer has to do to prepare his home. If I give my customer unreasonable work orders, it is my fault when our communication turns intermittent and poisonous.

What happens when I give my customer a time frame and three to five doable tasks?

The tasks are accomplished, and my customer and I succeed together in our listing preparation and time lines.

Now I can leave the walk-through armed with information that wins the forthcoming listing.

PART IV

SECOND
PHONE
CALL

When do I make my listing presentation?

I remember that the easy, simple, and comfortable path is the one the customer chooses.

So I will make her decision easy, simple, and comfortable, and she will choose me. I will present to my customers after my competitors. If there are three other bidders, I will go third. If two presentations are expected, mine will be the second. In this way, when the customer has reached the end of her interview process, the easy thing to do is bring it to an end by choosing me!

My customer begins the search for a real estate broker critically. Like all animals, human beings naturally seek safety. My customer knows the marketplace is filled with liars, thieves, and scoundrels. *When she begins her search, she is primarily scared of choosing the scoundrel. This fear occupies her mind and blinds her to other pursuits.*

When my customer interviews any broker, including me, she has doubts. Acting out of fear and self-preservation, she is specifically looking for signs of deception. In the first interview, the customer has doubts. In the second interview, the customer has doubts. By the time the customer interviews me, her last option, time has changed her decision paradigm; she no longer has the daylight to entertain multitudes of doubts. By the time she talks to me, she is no longer looking for the liar but someone she can trust. Her last option must be her best, else the time-consuming job of choosing a broker continues!

I will present last. By doing this, I multiply the odds I will be hired tenfold.

A simple strategy that will increase my income!

If I present first, the customer knows she has more options after me. During my presentation she is at her most critical. She is blinded by self-preservation and remembers primarily my potential misrepresentations.

If I present second, the customer knows she has more time to choose a broker. Additionally, now my presentation will be conglomerated with the first in her mind for a combined comparison with the last presentation—the one that will win!

When I present third, the customer is out of daylight, done with doubt, and excited to choose a camping spot. I refuse to present first!

I will present last. There will be no compromise to this strategy.

Successful negotiation is primarily dictated by position, not words. What general chooses the low ground over the high ground? None. If I negotiate from the low ground, I will inevitably be overrun.

I choose the high ground. I will present last. I will take an easy step to guarantee my success. I will set myself up for victory.

Presenting last makes my job easy. I choose the high ground.

I will present last.

Where is the listing presentation?

Where does an attorney, doctor, financial consultant, insurance agent, physical trainer, nutritionist, or mechanic meet his or her customer?

At the office, the same place every professional in the world meets their customers.

I will not give my listing presentation in my customer's home. I will not rob them of the chance to be focused, informed, and deliberate. I will allow them impartial ground to make smart decisions and create wealth. *To do otherwise is immoral.*

In my customer's home, on his or her turf, emotion rightfully guides decision making. Emotion, though, does not provide the winning mind-set for the seller.

In the home we are interrupted by the dog, the neighbor, and the leaking roof. In the home the customer is reminded of every task he has ever done to maintain the house. **In the home the customer does not have the capacity to think about the market: the entire collection of everyone *else's* homes!**

I will tell my customer the listing presentation will be at my office, and I will settle for nothing else. If I cannot negotiate this, I am doomed.

When my customer begs me to choose another venue—"I don't have time! I need to meet at the coffee shop!"—I smile and respond with, "When *do you* have time to talk about hundreds of thousands of dollars?"

I showed respect for their home in the walk-through, now they will come to my office for a listing presentation. This is a fair trade.

To allow it anywhere else hands the listing to my competition. My peer will eat, and I will go hungry, if I do not take home-field advantage.

How long is the listing presentation?

Forty-five minutes. No more.

One minute more, and I have lost.

The walk-through is forty-five minutes, so the listing presentation is forty-five minutes.

With a time constraint both my customer and I will succeed. Without a time constraint, we will waste time. Minutes will be wasted on social conversation. Minutes will be wasted on distractions. Minutes will be wasted on unimportant details.

The priceless moments of our lives will be wasted. Worse, these wasteful moments will inhibit successfully selling the home. These wasteful moments create a wasteful relationship.

With a time constraint, my customer will show up on time. If he does not, he will learn that my time is valuable. Without time constraints, it is my fault when my customer shows up late. It is my fault when this meeting makes me late for my next. It is my fault when I miss my workout because this meeting ran late. It is my fault when I miss dinner with my loved ones.

Without time constraints my customers will never have to be on time. They are less likely to answer my calls. They are more likely to call me in the evening on weekends. With time constraints they respect my time, my space, and my life. *They respect me.*

All decisions on this planet are forced by time. Without time constraints, no decisions would ever be reached, no buildings ever built.

Without hunger, we would not eat; without fatigue, we would not rest. The same is true with decisive action: without time constraints, there is no reason to actively proceed.

We show up late for things that are not important. This is not a yoga class. It is years of toil and accumulated wealth aggregated into a process I dictate! **Does this not warrant respect for the process?** Selling my customer's house is important. *It will impact his financial future more than any other decision he makes!* He must show up on time.

If I do not make my customer show up on time, I set us up for failure. My peers will sign and sell listings around me. Next, they will take my customer when I cannot sell his home!

Why did I not sell his home? Because my customer didn't listen to what I advised, because he didn't respect me, and *because I didn't demand a respectful relationship.*

I will confirm a forty-five-minute appointment, and I will keep it. NO MORE.

No matter how many rings on his fingers or awards on his walls, my customer will respect me when I set up a respectful relationship. Then we will be successful together.

We are successful together today because of one simple rule: my listing presentation will be forty-five minutes long.

SECTION
TWO

The
Listing
Presentation

PART V

LISTING
PRESENTION
PREPARATION

How is the listing presentation delivered?

Studies show approximately 92 percent of customers utilize the Internet when buying a home.

This is preposterous. What do the other 8 percent use? Cave paintings? **All relevant real estate marketing for my purposes is electronic. All of it.**

One hundred percent of real estate shoppers use the Internet. They all view online photos, use real estate search sites, and utilize online property information.

How can I verbally, or in writing, explain and demonstrate this electronic Internet marketing? I cannot. When I teach a child "apple," I put an apple in his hands. Explaining "apple," via words, writing, or images on paper is humorously less effective than simply placing an apple in his hands. I will demonstrate my electronic marketing as it exists, not as I could otherwise "explain" it.

I present to my customer in a private conference room at my office. I make my presentation on a flat-screen television linked to my computer. There is no paper; I am using Hollywood-quality imagery, sound, and video to show my customer how we will sell his or her home.

---

5   2014 Profile of Home Buyers and Sellers, National Association of Realtors, page 6.

To explain my marketing is to throw words into the wind.

To show my customer my marketing is to put a castle in their hands.

I will present to my customer in a private conference room on a large television screen.

I will think of a movie theater when I set up my conference room. I will shut the door. I will arrange seats in front of the television. I will make sure the lighting allows for an optimum viewing experience. I will block out distracting sounds. *The private screening theater is my model.*

In my conference room, as in a movie theater, the customers will relax. Once they relax, they will focus. Once they focus, they will decide. **This is a hierarchy: relaxation precedes focus and focus precedes decision. It is my job to prepare this victory.** Without allowing my customer to relax and focus, they cannot decide. It is my job to create this theater.

When I set up a poor learning environment, my words are lost, my ideas misunderstood, and my pitch forgotten. I fail. No matter how "right" I am, I fail.

I do not allow my peers, my company, or my schedule to dictate a poor meeting venue. When the conference room is in use, I wait. If there is no flat-screen TV in my conference room, I will buy one today.

If my peers do not present in a formal environment, then I will stand out as the clear choice.

When I present in a conference room, I control the message, just like a great movie director. I control the feelings. I control the meeting. The great director does not "explain" her movies, she shows them!

I have a private conference room with a flat-screen TV available for my listing presentation. I do not present my most important pitch casually.

How do I create the listing presentation?

The listing presentation will be created in a word-processing program (Apple Pages or Microsoft Word). I will display the document, page by page, on a large, flat-screen television in a conference room:

The Price Presentation (how to present this portion of the presentation is in steps 15–18)

Page 1: A page with my logo that reads:
"Listing Presentation for the _____ (fill in the blank) Family. Thank you for the opportunity to work for you."

Page 2: A page that reads "What Is My Price?" in large, bold letters (explained in step 15).

Page 3: The price, in large, bold letters (explained in step 15).

Page 4: Hyperlinks to three properties for use to justify the price (explained in step 16).

The Marketing Presentation (how to present this portion of the presentation is in steps 19–24)

Page 5: A page that reads, in large, bold letters, "Marketing Presentation," with a high-quality image of a high-end home (explained in step 20).

Page 6: A page that reads "Professional Photography" with three high-quality listing photos (explained in step 20).

Page 7: A page with three very low-quality photos (explained in step 20).

Page 8: A page that reads "Electronic Marketing," with hyperlinks to three listings on three different "sweeping" sites (explained in step 21).

Page 9: A page with hyperlinks to three "nonsweeping" sites (explained in step 21).

Page 10: A page with hyperlinks to three examples of social media exposure of my business or my listings (explained in step 21).

Page 11: A page that reads "Brokers' Open Houses and Open Houses," with a high-quality image of people eating at a restaurant (explained in step 22).

Page 12: A page that reads "Signage," with a high-quality image of your or your company's signage. (This page does not warrant explanation; it is shown to my customer to reinforce my branding.)

My Résumé Presentation (how to present this portion of the presentation is in step 23)

Page 13: A page that reads "Résumé" with hyperlinks to three public displays of my life, my job, or my company, though not necessarily the homes I have sold (to be explained in step 23).

Page 14: A page with my logo that reads "Thank you for your time, _____ family, I look forward to working for you."

GIVING THE LISTING PRESENTATION:

The price presentation

When do I deliver the price?

*Presenting pages 2, 3, and 4 of the
listing presentation from step 14*

The first thing I do in the presentation is present my customer with the price.

I present it in large text in an Apple Pages or Microsoft Word document as follows:

Your Listing Price is:
$525,000

I present the price first because price is the loosened cork in a champagne bottle; everyone is nervous before the cork pops. Price is the single most anticipated piece of information for the seller. Any conversation we have before the price delivery will be forgotten because the seller is anxiously awaiting…the **price**. To withhold the delivery of the price is to tell my children they must open their gifts the day *after* Christmas. My children would be blinded by insane anticipation to any concept besides opening their presents.

If I deliver the price first in the presentation, the customers' anxiety will have reached its summit immediately. From there, their discomfort level decreases throughout the course of the meeting until they have reached a state of emotional calm again. **This is how they must feel if I expect them to sign any paperwork.**

Conversely, if I present the price last, or near the end of the meeting, I will not have sufficient time to bring their emotional comfort level back to stasis.

Most sellers will be receiving a price suggestion that is less than they had expected. I recognize this, and I claim the time I need to educate them regarding price.

I give the customers what they want, and I give it to them immediately. I divulge their price first in the listing presentation.

By doing this, not only do I stand the best chance of signing the listing *at* the meeting, I also have the best chance of getting the correct listing price. If I accomplish both of these things, I will sell this house. I will sell it for the highest and best price, the transaction will be as simple as it can be, and the customer will be ecstatic.

If I fail to sign the listing at the right price, I expose myself to a high probability of losing it.

If I sign the listing, but get the wrong price, the customer will accumulate market time, likely receive substandard offers, be subject to comprehensive inspection processes, and be terribly, terribly, terribly stressed. If I am unlucky and unskilled, I may not get an offer at all. I will lose the listing and my confidence, and will have worked for free. Worst of all, I will have dried the river of future listing and sale opportunities by shutting it off at the source.

I can avoid this by simply presenting the price first.

I present the price first. I deflate built-up anticipation and stress; I topple discomfort. I lead my customers to the right price and the right decision. Their homes will be sold, and they will tell their peers about me. In this way, presenting the price first is a stupidly simple trick that is actually the key to a successful real estate sales career.

I give the price first.

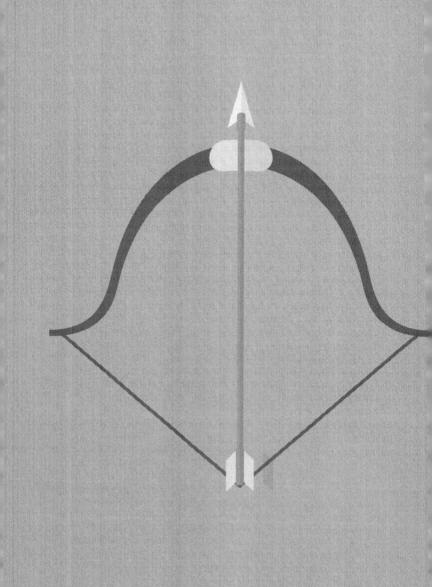

How do I prove the price?

*Presenting pages 2, 3, and 4 of the
listing presentation from step 14*

. . . .

When a stranger asks me the color of the sky, I point up.

Inevitably, I have answered him correctly!

Providing physical (on paper) market information, or a comparative market analysis or CMA, is embarrassingly antiquated. It is the easiest way to prove to a customer that my sales and marketing capacity is archaic.

Much worse, a paper CMA is less convincing then a photo of bigfoot; a CMA is easily refuted as poor evidence.

Should I provide my customer with a package of market information in paper format, they inevitably turn the pages irreverently, or discard it outright and say:

"That house is nothing like mine; the kitchen was small."

"Those people don't have a view."

"The owner didn't take care of that yard."

"Really?" I say.

"Consider this evidence:"

Then I provide my customer with high-quality photos of the massive kitchen, the panoramic view, and the immaculate landscape of the comparable sale. Thus ends that attempt to debunk the correct price.

My customer irrationally battles weak arguments that would make him poorer.

So, I choose a stronger weapon. I choose visual proof.

The photos are a mandatory and perfect weapon of my trade. I will continuously discharge them. If my customer thinks their home is worth $625,000 instead of $525,000, I show them a $625,000 kitchen.

I present three comparable sales visually on my flat-screen television using hyperlinks. I *show* the sold listings on the screen and guide the customer through the presentation with my cursor. I *show* the customer the main photo of the house, then the address, then the closing price. Next, and most importantly, I *show* the customer photos of the home that support the correct price.

As I show these photos of a comparable sale, the proof is evident and provided by a neutral nonhuman source; it is objective and scientific. While showing my customer photos of the comparable sales I have chosen, *I limit my talking.* Here the proof is evident, not subjective and coming from the experience of one single human being. *I establish a logical, inarguable testament to price using irrefutable proof.*

I prove the price by *showing* my customer three comparable closed sales using hyperlinks to the listing information.

I show them only three, because less information is more in this case. I do not entangle the strands of my customers' brain with endless information. They need to see good, solid proof quickly, and that is all. No more, no less.

Does my customer's opinion matter?

Presenting pages 2, 3, and 4 of the
listing presentation from step 14

My customer can easily choke on a grizzly piece of information. Next, by no fault of their own, they cannot breathe; they cannot ingest more information.

"Did that make sense?"

There are many ways to check in with the customer. I hold steadfast in doing this. No matter how confident I feel, no matter how likely it is I will win the listing, I promise myself I will constantly check in with my customer.

"Is this clear?"

I make sure to ask my customers what questions they have about the pricing presentation at all steps. I ask them throughout and after the presentation.

"Is what you're seeing making sense?"

My customers must feel that I care about them and their success. As I check in, I express that concern and also learn more about what satisfies them.

Additionally, I guarantee their ability to digest important information. My customers may sit quietly and patiently, seeming to internalize what I show them. Their accepting demeanor, however, can easily belie confusion. If my customers become confused regarding a particular topic, we can clarify it and proceed.

When I check in with my customers, I witness magical transformations. The grumpy person becomes happy, the confused person, deliberate, and the doubtful person, trusting. Our successful relationship hinges on mutual success, so I will always check in with my customers.

If I do not, they may be sitting beside me choking, blocked from a conversation that would otherwise forge our path.

My mountain is formed of molten trust, and this I gain today by asking simply:

"Does this make sense?"

Can I ask my customer to sign again...now?

What stands to be gained by postponing the signing process?

Nothing.

However, much can be lost.

There are more worries than stars in the sky, and I refuse to sit and ponder them when the customer is ready. We sign. Of course, there are more important details about the showing protocol, about how offers are made, and about how the sale process will occur. *All of these are significantly lower priorities than agreeing to a listing; I refuse to discuss them if my customer holds a pen!*

I sign the listing, share in the momentary celebration of a sound decision, and educate the customer further at a later point. My job is to sell the home *and* make the customer happy. **Anything that delays these outcomes is attempted defiance of the gravity of success. I cannot defy gravity.** When it is natural to succeed, I feel that pull, and I oblige. This is easy, and I heed it today.

If my customer is ready, so am I!

I ask my customer if he or she is ready to sign. ***If the answer is yes, we will sign an agreement.***

There is only one time when my query to sign listing paperwork is sorely misguided: if my customer is or has been discussing the death of a loved one. **At all other times, it is acceptable to ask the customer to sign listing paperwork.** Contrary to my fears and doubts, this strengthens the appearance of my professionalism to the customer. The listing agreement is complete, sitting next to me in a folder. I have highlighted all areas my customer needs to sign. I have written the dates for them next to where they need to sign. The paperwork is arranged in order: the longest, most arduous documents first, and the shortest, easiest documents last.

When I am hungry I eat; when I am tired, I sleep.

My customer also abides the laws of energy. When she is ready to move forward, we move forward.

If the customer is ready to sign, we will sign the agreement that day!

I will not discourage her.

I ask my customer to sign. Routinely. I will hear yes.

PART VII

GIVING THE LISTING PRESENTATION:

The marketing presentation

Can I omit the marketing presentation?

Whether or not my customer has already signed listing paperwork, there *is* marketing information to share.

If my customer has already signed listing paperwork, I will quickly educate them about how, when, and where they will see their listing. This is the language used to present pages 8 and 9 of the listing presentation:

There are two types of real estate websites (this explains "sweeping" and "nonsweeping" listing sites from step 14); **those that automatically sweep/upload my listing, and those that do not.**

1. The "sweeping" sites will automatically upload the listing and corrections to the listing within forty-eight hours. Examples of these sites are Keller Williams, RE/MAX, Brookshire Hathaway, and Century 21, and there are literally thousands of others. All brokers' listings appear on these international sweeping sites.

2. I will upload the listing to all relevant "nonsweeping" sites within 48 hours. Examples of these sites are Zillow and Trulia, though there are thousands of others. By uploading the listing to Zillow and Trulia, in addition to creating automatic listings on the sweeping sites, I have essentially marketed the property to the entire world. **Many brokers do not upload to the nonsweeping sites, effectively "halving" their listings market exposure. This is a gross miscalculation that stunts the sale.**

For the actual listing to appear online, the errors to be caught, and the revised version to be posted can take up to forty-eight hours. It is important my customers understand the timing of these events to assuage their anxiety. The customers simply need to be patient. And they will be, because I tell them what to expect!

By preparing my customer, I validate my professionalism and set the backdrop for a smooth, low-stress, and efficient transaction. If I do not prepare my customer for how, when, and where they will find their listing, I will receive up to five confused phone calls, e-mails, or text messages per week. By taking approximately thirty seconds to prepare my customer, I save us two hours of frustration.

I understand that preparing my customer creates a powerful, trust-filled relationship. Every time I tell my customer what will happen, and it happens, I grow trust and strengthen our professional relationship. The roots of our powerful relationship extend far from the base of our tree in this way. Strong winds do not affect us.

The single most important dynamic of a winning relationship with a customer is thorough preparation. This is a high-level practice of communication. The results of the transaction are less important than preparing the customers for the possible results. I do not like to be surprised, and my customer does not like to be surprised; therefore, I commit to doing my best to prepare my customer.

My customer may want to leave the meeting early, in a hurry to do something far less important than make a large financial decision. I will not let this occur. If we have signed the paperwork, but we have not covered the basics of Internet marketing, when they say, "OK we are done, right?"

I will reply, "No. I need you to understand the next thing I tell you so you remain happy during our transaction."

I will not allow my customer to leave in haste only to have him or her chastise me later for a frustration that can be avoided. Instead, I will prepare my customer—and I will magically predict the future.

Are professional listing photos important?

Presenting pages 5, 6, and 7 of the
listing presentation from step 14

What moment signifies the beginning of our lives?

The first time we open our eyes.

At what moment does a mother experience true love?

When she makes eye contact with her child.

When we take our final breaths, what moment do we all agree signifies the end?

When we close our eyes.

We are visually centered animals. Our sight is our primary, favorite, and most alluring sense. I remember this at all times when I am searching for, meeting with, and serving my customer. Most of all, I remember this when I secure their riches for them by marketing their real estate. **I will hire professional graphic artists to shoot and enhance my photos. I will get more showings, and I will sell listings faster and for a higher price. This is my moral obligation.**

All important events call for important presentations. The sale of my customers' home may be the most important single financial event of their lives. I diminish the perceived value of their investment if I using substandard, nonprofessional photography.

Professional photos cost $250.

The use of professional photos for the listing fetches my customer a higher sale price—up to a 3 percent increase.

The photographer uses sophisticated lenses and computer programs to make the home appear as spacious, bright, and warm as possible. His images will be swept by thousands of websites to hundreds of thousands of people worldwide. **This is my entire pool of potential buyers!** They must be baited, not bored, by what they see. Only when these buyers have developed sufficient interest to see the home can I actually sell the home. These photos are my calling card.

By using nonprofessional photography I am absolutely and without question costing my seller real money. Subsequently, my efforts to sell my listings will be thwarted, and my business will suffer.

Any listing, any price range, any scenario—I always use professional photography.

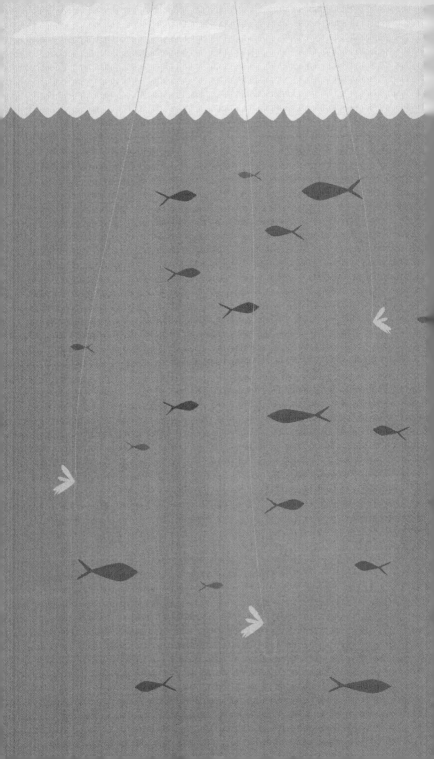

How do I explain electronic Internet marketing?

Presenting pages 8, 9, and 10 of the listing presentation from step 14

Buyers use the Internet to find their homes. They may casually peruse magazines, newspapers, and fliers, but they all return to the Internet to shop, because all buyers go through a buying stage of "comparison;" they want to know that they are getting the best value. The way they gauge value is by comparing what they like against other comparable listings. The most comprehensive sources are MLS sweeping sites, not a metal rack at the supermarket.

All buyers use the Internet.

Now is when I show page 8 of my listing presentation, after I have explained the above. I then demonstrate, on the screen in front of me, three different MLS sweeping sites my listings appear on. The listings I choose, of course, have high-quality, professional photos.

Next I show page 9, demonstrating three examples of high-quality listings on nonsweeping sites (Zillow and Trulia). Here I take time to explain the vitality of uploading my listings to all relevant nonsweeping sites:

"Electronic real estate marketing is fishing for the sweetest, cleanest, sushi-grade fish; there are a lot of lines in the water, with the best bait. This process guarantees the highest probability of landing the best fish, the best buyer, in your marketplace".

Now, showing page 10, I demonstrate how exhaustively I use social media, blogs, and any other relevant media sources (e.g., my blog, my Facebook account, and my personal website).

When my customer sees the sheer volume of exposure I can provide for their listing, they cannot doubt my abilities. In fact, if they find a relevant source with which to list their real estate—one that I have not used—I will list there, too.

To feed my family, I put the most, and best, fishing lines in the water. Electronic Internet marketing is how buyers find homes, so this is where I cast my lines.

Do I use open houses?
Presenting page 11 of the listing
presentation from step 14

Studies regarding the efficacy of open houses vary widely in their results.
Depending on the source, open houses seem to have a positive effect on
a sale (creating a sale or creating a faster sale) 2 percent to 20 percent
of the time. That is to say, 80 percent to 98 percent of sales are not
affected by an open house. What are these other people doing on private
property? In the safest case, they were hoping for a free meal.

The king's share of homes do not sell as a result of open houses. I refuse to
allow 80 percent of my time and energy with a seller be unduly annexed
by a practice that produces, at best, 20 percent higher chance of success.

I will do anything it takes to sell my customers' homes—anything.
But we all realize that we have limited time to accomplish this
important feat.

By the Pareto principle, or the 80–20 rule, 20 percent of my activities
dictate 80 percent of my success. I refuse to include unproven tools in
my toolbox.

Open houses may or may not be beneficial to me, depending where
I am at in my career and what my values are. They can grow my
business, market my name, and introduce me to new customers. That
much is true.

But open houses are not a mandatory part of my success. In the extreme case, they introduce dozens of ill-intended strangers into my customers' most private of places; this risk must be considered.

I will do anything to sell my customers' homes, including open houses, but only if that event has a viable chance of creating a sale.

PART VIII

GIVING THE LISTING LISTING PRESENTATION:

My résumé presentation

How do I present my résumé?

*Presenting page 13 of the listing
presentation from step 14*

The same way any accomplished and confident professional would:
humbly.

My life is a collection of wondrous relationships, memories, and
achievements. So many, in fact, they are too numerous to recount. As
a professional, or any established individual, I will appear arrogant if I
recount my entire résumé!

So, first, to preemptively deflate a perception of hubris, I make them
laugh at me. *I use a graphic that depicts my business or myself in a
humorous or creative manner.*

Second, I plot all sales, listings, co-listings and any real estate
transactions I have completed on a map. I will show the map as it
relates to my seller's property; their property will be the center of the
graphic. I know that seeing is believing, so I will show my customer my
expertise in their locale.

*If I do not have sufficient sales to show a winning map to my customer, I
will consult chapter 24.*

Finally, I show my customer three testimonials. The testimonials will
reference exactly who made the statement, by first and last name
and by neighborhood. If I have no real estate experience, character
references suffice.

I have listened to my customers, now they want to know more about me. I will give them real visuals, as listed above, to prove to them I am a real professional with real results for real people. Any "telling" regarding my success or my sales will likely be ignored; again, words mean little compared to visuals.

Should my customer interrupt the presentation of my résumé and request to sign paperwork, I will happily oblige. There is no fact about myself that is integral to this sale—not one. When the customer is sold on my service and ready to sign, I will forget my personal presentation and move forward. **I will remember, above all else, that this process is about the customer first.** My needs are a distant second, if they exist at all, until I succeed in selling my customer's home.

Again, I will seek my customer's signatures on a signed agreement. Once we have succeeded together, then I have earned the right to discuss my needs: referrals.

What if I am not qualified?

If my customer has not signed, and if I have any doubt as to whether they will, I have one powerful rocket yet to fire: **the ownership of my frailty, failure, and humanity.**

I have not won a championship!
So my hunger is greater than he who has won five. My eyes are glued to a trophy held in my hands in the future.

I have never sold a house!
Please show me who is more motivated to make this sale than I! She who has sold one hundred homes is fed; I am hungry. Who will commit to your goals, your success, your sale? Me. I have no option but to succeed for you!

Here is the grandest irony of sales:

Ownership of my own frailty, my deepest insecurity, my dearth of skills is the most powerful sales weapon that exists. **That which my peer uses as gossip is my greatest strength.**

I will admit to my deficiency and use that as my greatest asset.

If I have four deficiencies, I have four great assets:

I am old = I am wise.

I am scared = I am alert.

I am frail = I look constantly to gain strength.

I do not know = I will learn!

When I own and accept my failures, I have no option but to unleash my primal ability to run, to fight, and to achieve. I remember that my bloodline is the product of over five hundred million years of the universe assaulting life on earth. In the deepest places of my soul, in every cell in my body, I am born of grand triumph. How far can the farthest telescopes seek life and not find me?

They will not find me!

I own my past and my failures, and I fill my tank with their fuel.

Today I succeed, because I must.

"These, sir, are the reasons I must have your business, and the reasons I must succeed for you. Failure is not in my DNA."

How can this declaration be denied?

How do I seek the "close" after the meeting?

I will call the customer until she makes a decision. If the customer tells me when I can call her back, I will accommodate her wish. If the customer does not tell me when I should call her back, I will call her every other day.

There is no script for making a sale.

There is no script for making a sale.

There is no script for making a sale.

If there were a perfect script, robots, not humans, would sell homes. I realize that anytime I use canned language on my customer, they feel like tuna. No one wants to buy from a robot. My customer wants to buy from someone who is qualified—someone they like and trust. I am myself when I call my customer.

I employ these techniques to win the sale:

1. I will persist as sure as the sun. My golden rays will not stop shining. I will not stop trying. My peers fail not for lack of skill, but lack of commitment.

2. I remind the customer why she thinks the house will not sell. The customer shared this information with me at the walk-through *(see step 8)*.

3. I prescribe the remedy for this challenge.

3. I sell my inadequacies to the customer so that she will know my humanity. This cannot be rejected.

4. I will thank my customer for the opportunity to work. We are not owed work; we are lucky to have it. I will never forget this fact, and my customer will know my gratitude for this opportunity.

5. I will politely but persistently ask if the customer is prepared to sell her house (to sign paperwork).

Most important, when I enter my office every day I note the weather. I study the sky. I smell the air. I listen to the birds. Every day, the weather is different. Sometimes it's hospitable and soft; sometimes it's harsh. The weather reminds me that all things on this planet change constantly. My customer is a child of the weather, and also its imitator; she changes daily.

I know that if I persist earnestly, and if I continue to refine my pitch, my customer will one day be receptive. I refuse to quit until we have reached that day.

MANDATORY READING LIST:

Mandino, Og. *The Greatest Salesman in the World.*
New York: Bantam, 1993.

Peale, Norman Vincent. *The Power of Positive Thinking.*
New York: Fireside, 1980.

Tracy, Brian. *The Psychology of Selling.*
Nashville: Thomas Nelson, 2004.

Keller, Gary and Jay Papasan. *The ONE Thing.*
Austin: Bard Press, 2013.

Keller, Gary. *The Millionaire Real Estate Agent.*
New York: McGraw-Hill, 2004.

Hill, Napoleon. *Think and Grow Rich.*
Seattle: Pacific Publishing Studio, 2009.

Pink, Daniel H. *Drive: The Surprising Truth About What Motivates Us.*
New York: Riverhead Books, 2009.

Thank you for reading this book.

Please share your real estate sales secret at:

www.mattcparker.com

34261468R00070

Made in the USA
Middletown, DE
14 August 2016